USBORNE BIG MACHINES
PLANES
AND HELICOPTERS

Clive Gifford

Designed by Steve Page

Illustrated by Mark Franklin
Additional illustrations by Sean Wilkinson
Cover design by Tom Lalonde

Consultant: L.F.E. Coombs (transport writer)

Contents

Many thanks to Airbus Industrie, British Aerospace, Andy Bounce, Canadair Group of Bombardier, Inc.,
Richard Goode Aerobatic Displays, Bill Goodliffe, Lockheed Corporation, Martin Baker Aircraft Co. Ltd.,
Sloane Helicopters Ltd., Westland Helicopters Ltd., Adrian Wigham

Planes in flight

Planes are lifted into the air by their engines and wings. Moving flaps on the tail and wings help the plane change direction. These flaps are called control surfaces.

The flaps on the tailplanes are called elevators.

This flap on the tail is called the rudder.

These little wings at the back of the plane are called tailplanes.

The flap on the wing is called an aileron.

This plane is a Cessna 150. It comes from the United States.

This is where the pilot sits. It is called the cockpit.

The engine turns the propeller. The propeller pulls the plane through the air.

The wheels and the parts which join them to the plane are called the undercarriage.

Planes used by armies and navies are called military planes. All others are known as civil planes.

What the control surfaces do

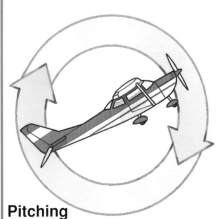

Pitching

The elevators make the plane go up and down. This is called pitching.

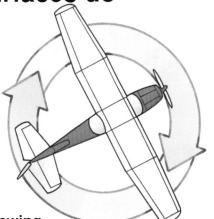

Yawing

The rudder makes the plane go left or right. This is called yawing.

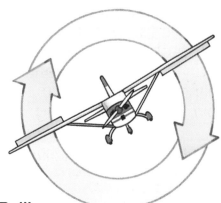

Rolling

The ailerons tip the plane from side to side. This is called rolling.

Carrying passengers

Planes transport people all over the world. This plane can carry up to 110 passengers and their bags. It is called a British Aerospace 146.

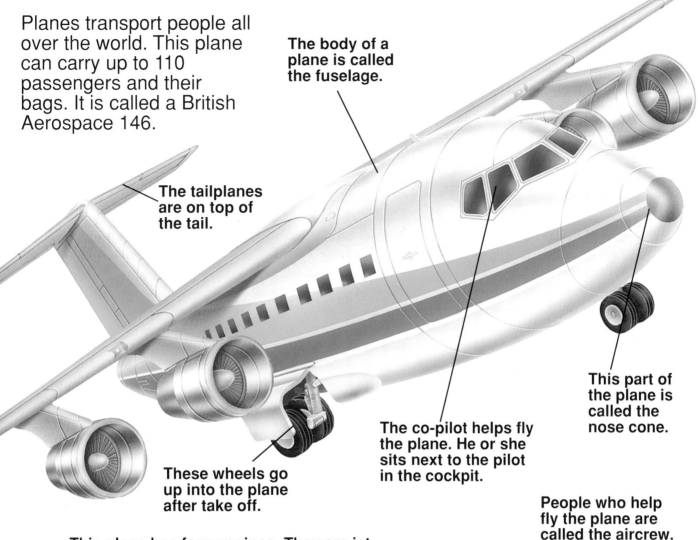

The body of a plane is called the fuselage.

The tailplanes are on top of the tail.

This part of the plane is called the nose cone.

The co-pilot helps fly the plane. He or she sits next to the pilot in the cockpit.

People who help fly the plane are called the aircrew.

These wheels go up into the plane after take off.

This plane has four engines. They are jet engines which push the plane forward.

Inside the cockpit

The cockpit contains all the controls the pilot needs to fly the plane. There are many dials and screens telling the pilot and co-pilot how the plane is doing.

Radio

This is the control column. It makes the ailerons and elevators move.

These are called the rudder pedals because they move the tail's rudder. The pilot controls them with his feet.

Maps can be stored here.

3

Helicopters

Helicopters are machines which fly by using rotors. Rotors are thin wings which spin around very fast. These spinning rotors move the helicopter through the air.

These are the main rotor blades. They do all the work of lifting the helicopter up into the air. This helicopter has four of them.

Here are seats for three passengers.

With the door open you can see the cockpit.

Dials and screens tell the pilot how to fly. They are all found in this box called the instrument panel.

These are rudder pedals.

Many helicopters do not have wheels. This helicopter rests on the ground on long, flat blades called skids.

The cabin door slides back.

This lever controls how high the helicopter flies. It is called the collective pitch control.

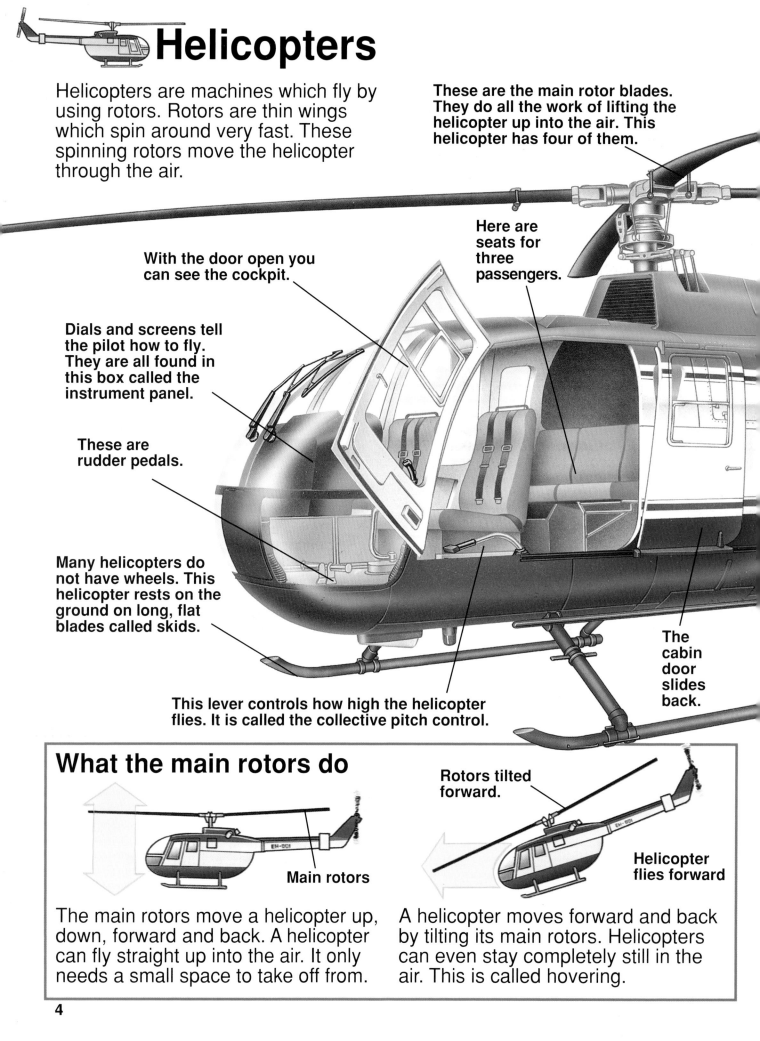

What the main rotors do

Main rotors

Rotors tilted forward.

Helicopter flies forward

The main rotors move a helicopter up, down, forward and back. A helicopter can fly straight up into the air. It only needs a small space to take off from.

A helicopter moves forward and back by tilting its main rotors. Helicopters can even stay completely still in the air. This is called hovering.

4

This is a German helicopter called an MBB-105.

Here is the tail rotor. It helps the helicopter change direction.

Left or right

The tail rotor steers the helicopter left or right. It is controlled by the rudder pedals.

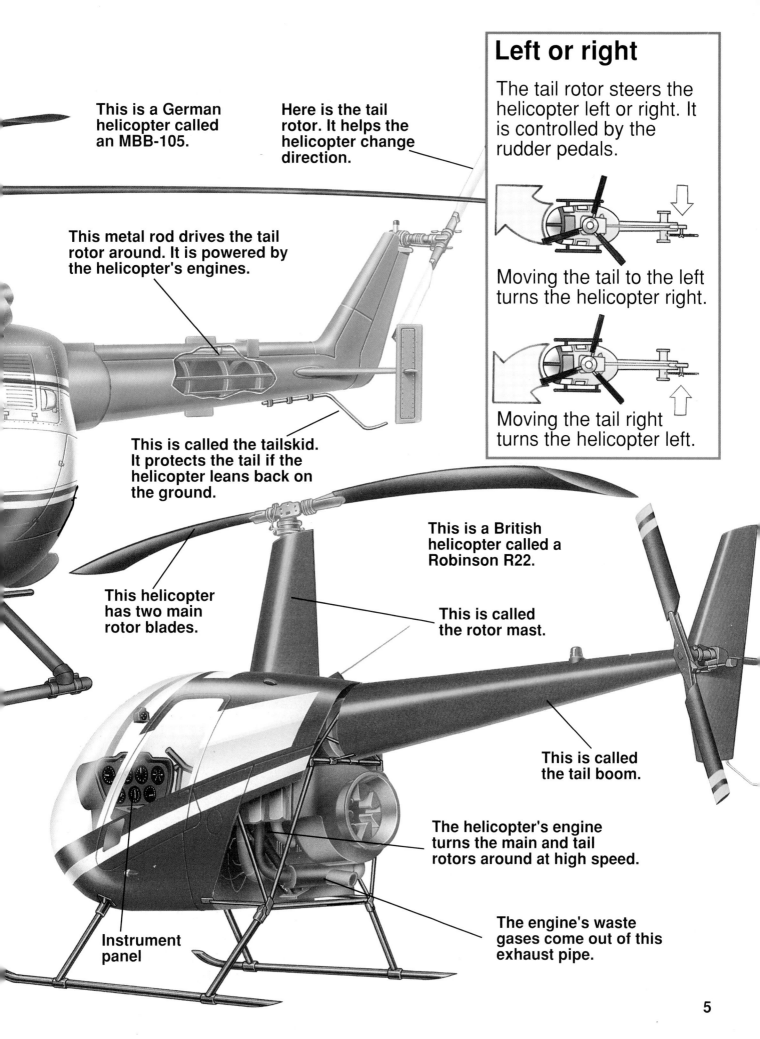

Moving the tail to the left turns the helicopter right.

Moving the tail right turns the helicopter left.

This metal rod drives the tail rotor around. It is powered by the helicopter's engines.

This is called the tailskid. It protects the tail if the helicopter leans back on the ground.

This helicopter has two main rotor blades.

This is a British helicopter called a Robinson R22.

This is called the rotor mast.

This is called the tail boom.

The helicopter's engine turns the main and tail rotors around at high speed.

Instrument panel

The engine's waste gases come out of this exhaust pipe.

Historic planes

The first plane flew in 1903. Since then, hundreds of different planes have been built. Here are four famous old planes.

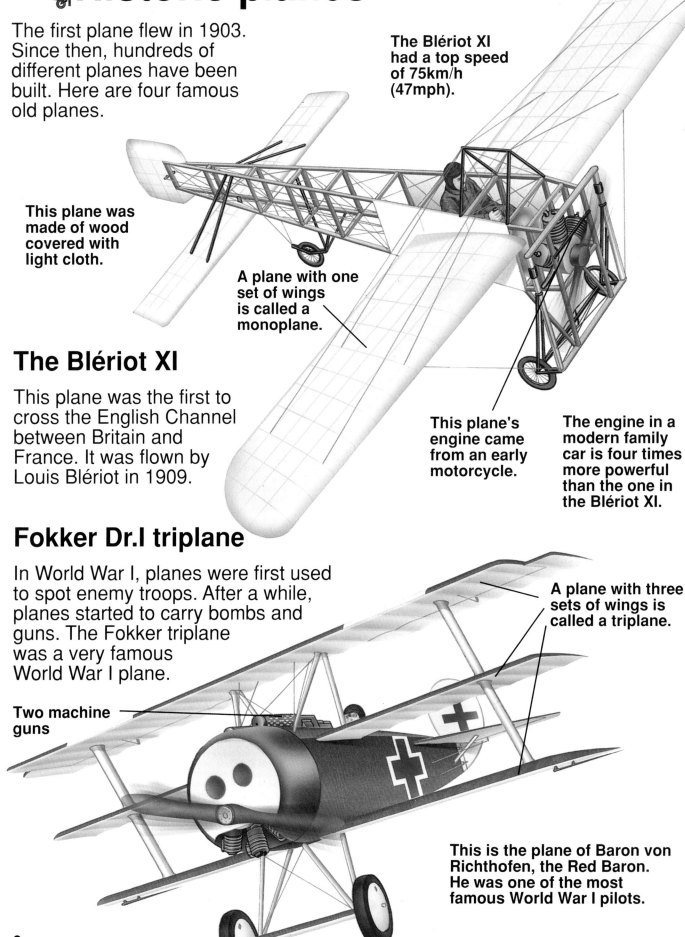

The Blériot XI had a top speed of 75km/h (47mph).

This plane was made of wood covered with light cloth.

A plane with one set of wings is called a monoplane.

The Blériot XI

This plane was the first to cross the English Channel between Britain and France. It was flown by Louis Blériot in 1909.

This plane's engine came from an early motorcycle.

The engine in a modern family car is four times more powerful than the one in the Blériot XI.

Fokker Dr.I triplane

In World War I, planes were first used to spot enemy troops. After a while, planes started to carry bombs and guns. The Fokker triplane was a very famous World War I plane.

A plane with three sets of wings is called a triplane.

Two machine guns

This is the plane of Baron von Richthofen, the Red Baron. He was one of the most famous World War I pilots.

Dragon Rapide

This plane first flew in 1934. It helped to make flying more popular and was used by many different airlines.

A plane with two sets of wings is called a biplane.

Inside there were seats for up to 16 people.

The Rapide's normal, or cruising, speed was not much faster than the top speed of a modern family car.

The Rapide's two engines were built into the wing.

Gloster Meteor

The Gloster Meteor was one of the first warplanes to be powered by a jet engine. It was built in Britain and first flew near the end of World War II.

The first Meteors had a top speed of 625km/h (385mph).

Gases were forced out of the back of the engine, which pushed the plane forward.

The Meteor had a jet engine built into each wing.

Airliners

Planes that carry a lot of passengers are called airliners.

This is the passenger deck. This plane has seats for over 370 people.

This is a modern airliner called the Airbus A340.

Passengers can put small bags in these lockers above their seats.

The cockpit's windows are made of a mixture of glass and very tough plastic.

The plane's engines are very powerful but quieter than earlier jet engines.

These are called flaps. When they are down they make the wing bigger. This helps slow the plane down.

Computers in the cockpit

The A340's cockpit has lots of computer screens. They tell the pilot about the plane's height, speed and engines.

This screen tells the pilot if the plane is going up, down, left or right.

This screen shows a line called the artificial horizon. It tells the pilot if the plane is flying level.

A map is shown on this screen. This helps the pilot fly the plane in the right direction.

Control column

Throttles control the engines' speed.

Airbus A340

The Airbus A340 is a brand new airliner built by a group of European companies working together. It first flew in 1991. It is full of up-to-date equipment, like computers, inside.

The design of the company who owns the plane is painted along the body and on the tail. It is called the livery.

The A340's engines are joined to the wings by supports called pylons.

Here is where the passengers' bags are stored. It is called the luggage hold.

The A340 can travel from London to Chicago and back before it needs more fuel.

Tailplane

Loading and unloading

A big airliner must be loaded with many different things before it can take off.

This tanker fills the plane up with fuel.

A van pulls along trailers of luggage to be loaded.

This is the catering truck. It loads on all the food and drink needed for the flight.

The arms push the top part of the van up to the height of the plane to make loading easier.

This bus carries passengers and aircrew to and from the plane.

This tug pulls the airliner along when it is on the ground.

Passenger and aircrew steps

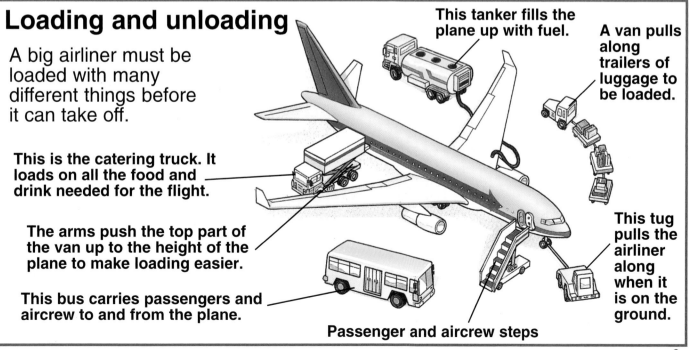

The fastest

The first planes and helicopters were slower than today's cars. As people learned more about how planes fly and built more powerful engines, planes got faster.

Concorde

Concorde is the fastest airliner ever. It has a top speed of over 2,300km/h (1,450mph). It can travel from New York to London in just under three hours.

Concorde can carry 100 passengers.

Lynx

This is the world's fastest helicopter. It has a top recorded speed of 400km/h (250mph).

North American X-15

This plane first flew in the 1960s. It still holds the record as the fastest plane in the world. It had a top speed of over 7000km/h (4,300mph). That is three times as fast as Concorde can fly today.

The X15 has a rocket engine, similar to the ones space rockets use.

The X15 had very short wings.

Most really fast planes, like the X15, have pointed noses.

A pointed nose helps a plane punch a hole through the air as it speeds forward.

The plane only had room for a single pilot.

SR-71 Blackbird

The SR71 first flew in 1965. It was built by the United States as a spy plane. It could fly very high and very fast. This meant that it could not be caught by other planes.

This plane can fly at one and a half times the speed of Concorde.

The Blackbird was used until 1990.

In the nose are cameras which can see a long way.

The cockpit has room for two people.

The plane flies so high that the pilot and co-pilot need special suits like an astronaut's.

Here is one of the Blackbird's very powerful engines.

This was one of the first jet planes to be painted black to make it hard to see. This is how it got its name of Blackbird.

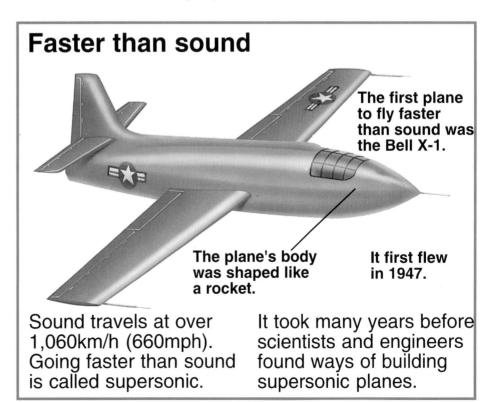

Faster than sound

The first plane to fly faster than sound was the Bell X-1.

The plane's body was shaped like a rocket.

It first flew in 1947.

Sound travels at over 1,060km/h (660mph). Going faster than sound is called supersonic.

It took many years before scientists and engineers found ways of building supersonic planes.

VTOL planes

VTOL stands for Vertical Take Off and Landing. A VTOL plane can fly straight up into the air without needing a runway. It uses powerful blasts of hot air and gases from its engine. Parts of the plane called thrusters point the blasts in different directions.

The pilot's right hand moves the control column.

The pilot's left hand controls which way the thrusters point.

In here, a special machine helps guide missiles to their target.

The Harrier

The Harrier is the best known VTOL plane. There are many models of Harrier. This one is called a GR7.

This light is used when the plane lands.

This front wheel is called the nosewheel.

The first VTOL plane

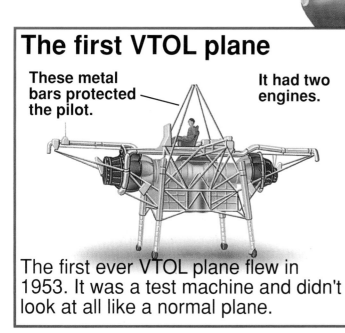

These metal bars protected the pilot.

It had two engines.

The first ever VTOL plane flew in 1953. It was a test machine and didn't look at all like a normal plane.

Thrusters

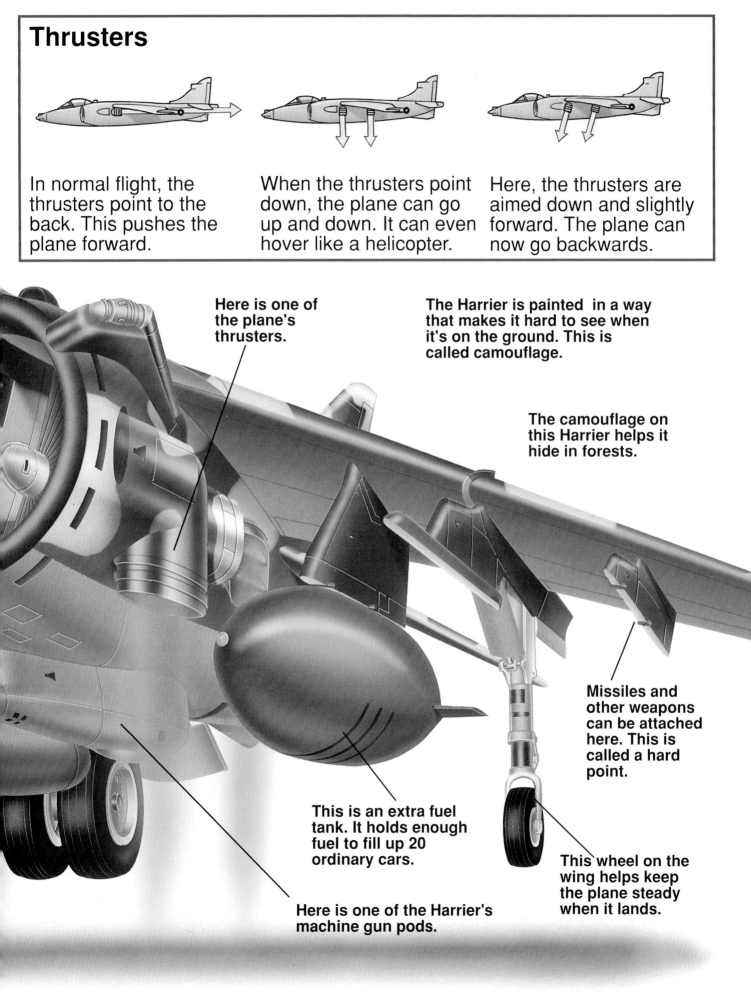

In normal flight, the thrusters point to the back. This pushes the plane forward.

When the thrusters point down, the plane can go up and down. It can even hover like a helicopter.

Here, the thrusters are aimed down and slightly forward. The plane can now go backwards.

Here is one of the plane's thrusters.

The Harrier is painted in a way that makes it hard to see when it's on the ground. This is called camouflage.

The camouflage on this Harrier helps it hide in forests.

Missiles and other weapons can be attached here. This is called a hard point.

This is an extra fuel tank. It holds enough fuel to fill up 20 ordinary cars.

Here is one of the Harrier's machine gun pods.

This wheel on the wing helps keep the plane steady when it lands.

Sea planes and float planes

Most planes need a runway on solid ground. Sea planes and float planes can use water instead. They can take off from and land on lakes and the sea.

Float planes

These planes have floats attached to their wings or underneath their body. The float plane below is called a De Havilland Beaver. It carries people and mail around countries, like Canada, which have many lakes.

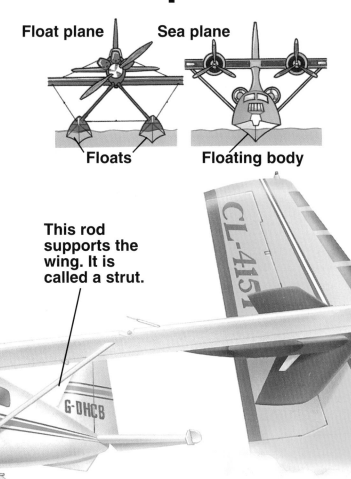

Float plane   Sea plane

Floats   Floating body

This rod supports the wing. It is called a strut.

This is one of the aircraft's floats.

The floats are filled with air and stop the plane from sinking.

This fin on the float is called a rudder. It helps steer the plane on the water.

The largest plane ever

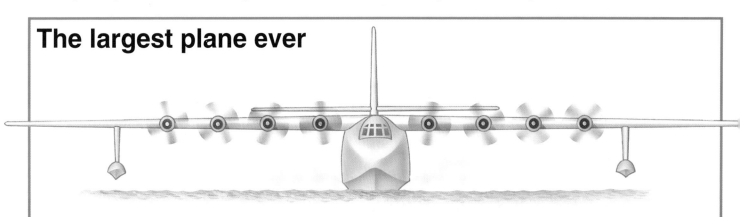

The Spruce Goose was a huge sea plane built in the 1940s. It was paid for by an American millionaire named Howard Hughes. It was the largest plane ever made. It had eight engines and a wingspan the length of a soccer field. In 1947 it made its only flight, a trip of 1.6km (1 mile).

Sea planes

A sea plane's body is called a hull. It is shaped like a boat and keeps the plane afloat on the water. This sea plane is called a Canadair CL-415. Its special job is putting out big fires.

The plane is brightly painted. This is so the fire fighters on the ground can see it coming and get clear before the plane drops its load of water.

This float on the end of the wing stops the plane from tipping over in the water.

This plane has wheels as well as floats so it can move on land as well as on water. Planes like this are called amphibians.

The two engines are on top of the wings.

C-FAWD

Canadair

This is the tank where the water for putting out fires is stored.

The hull has a curved shape to run through the water smoothly.

The water bomber

Water enters plane here.

Hatch opens

The CL-415 drops water 'bombs' on forest fires to help put them out. It gets the water by scooping it up as it skims over lakes or the sea.

In just 10 seconds it can collect enough water to fill 80 baths. It flies back to the fire and in a few seconds, dumps all of the water out of a big hatch in its body.

Cargo planes

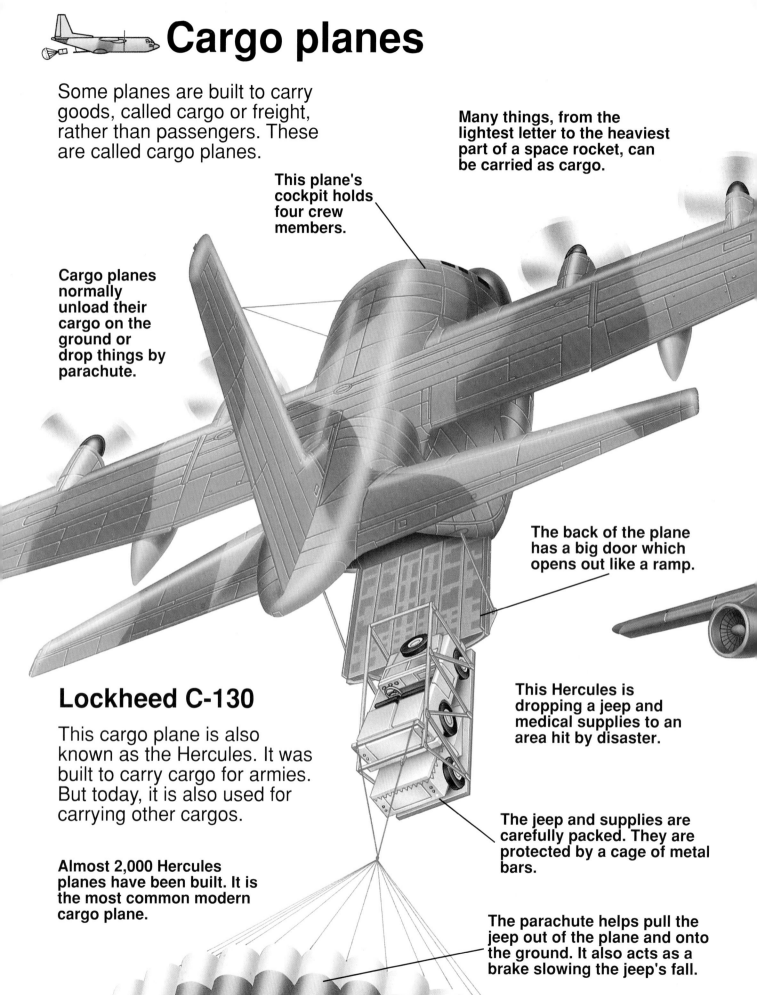

Some planes are built to carry goods, called cargo or freight, rather than passengers. These are called cargo planes.

Many things, from the lightest letter to the heaviest part of a space rocket, can be carried as cargo.

This plane's cockpit holds four crew members.

Cargo planes normally unload their cargo on the ground or drop things by parachute.

The back of the plane has a big door which opens out like a ramp.

Lockheed C-130

This cargo plane is also known as the Hercules. It was built to carry cargo for armies. But today, it is also used for carrying other cargos.

This Hercules is dropping a jeep and medical supplies to an area hit by disaster.

Almost 2,000 Hercules planes have been built. It is the most common modern cargo plane.

The jeep and supplies are carefully packed. They are protected by a cage of metal bars.

The parachute helps pull the jeep out of the plane and onto the ground. It also acts as a brake slowing the jeep's fall.

The nose lifts right up so that large things can easily be fitted inside.

MILITARY AIRLIFT COMMAND

Here is the cockpit

Here you can see the steps that go up to the cockpit.

The C-5 Galaxy

This plane carries military cargo. It is the biggest cargo plane flying today. It is more than twice as long as the Hercules.

This is the main cargo deck. It is over 4m (13.5ft) high and 34m (121ft) long.

This big ramp folds down after the nose has opened.

How much can it hold?

The Galaxy has an enormous body. It can easily hold three helicopters or six big trucks. Above the cargo deck, the Galaxy also has room for up to 75 soldiers and all their equipment.

Main cargo deck

Upper passenger deck.

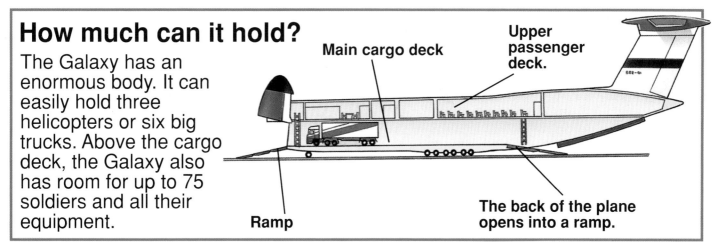

Ramp

The back of the plane opens into a ramp.

Helicopters at work

Helicopters are used for all sorts of jobs. They carry both passengers and cargo. They can fly in places where ordinary planes cannot. They are often used for rescue work.

Different jobs

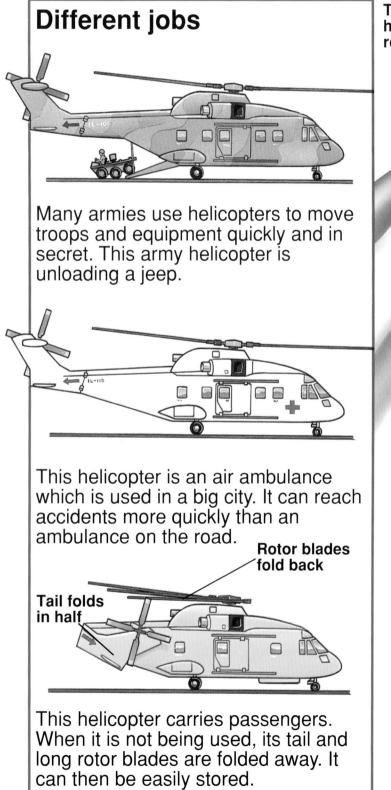

Many armies use helicopters to move troops and equipment quickly and in secret. This army helicopter is unloading a jeep.

This helicopter is an air ambulance which is used in a big city. It can reach accidents more quickly than an ambulance on the road.

Rotor blades fold back

Tail folds in half

This helicopter carries passengers. When it is not being used, its tail and long rotor blades are folded away. It can then be easily stored.

These are the helicopter's main rotor blades.

This is the tail rotor. It is 4m (13ft) from tip to tip.

This helicopter has three engines. If one breaks down, it can still fly safely on the other two.

This is the tail plane. It helps keep the helicopter steady.

This helicopter can carry 4,000kg (8,700lb) of cargo or 30 passengers.

The EH101

The EH101 was built by companies in Britain and Italy. It can be used for many different jobs.

The one shown here flies over the sea. Its job is to hunt for enemy ships and submarines.

These wipers keep the windows clear in rainy weather.

The pilot is given orders over a radio in his helmet.

This part of the helicopter is known as a sponson. Inside it you can see one of the helicopter's wheels.

The pilot wears a special suit which protects him from fire.

This bulge holds special equipment which searches for submarines below the sea's surface.

Aerobatic planes

Aerobatics are acrobatic moves that planes sometimes do. You can often see planes doing aerobatics at airshows. The pilots make the planes twist and turn in the sky.

Sukhoi Su-26

This Russian plane is specially built for aerobatics. It is made from modern materials and is very light and strong.

The undercarriage is made of a strong but light metal called titanium.

This pipe is where the gases from the engine leave the plane. It is called the exhaust pipe.

The gases are mixed with special chemicals to make lots of smoke trails for the crowd to watch.

This plane can roll all the way around every second.

The pilot must be very fit and strong. Aerobatic flying can be very tiring.

Stunt flying

Some planes do exciting tricks, called stunts, to entertain crowds. One popular stunt is wing walking. In fact, the person doesn't walk but is strapped tightly to the wing of a flying plane.

Wing walkers sometimes hold flags or wave to crowds.

These wires help hold the person in place.

This plane is called a Boeing Stearman. It is often used for wing walking.

The pilot does simple tricks with the plane. Some even do a loop the loop (see below).

Loops and rolls

There are many different moves in aerobatics. A pilot will try to link several moves together.

This is called a Cuban Eight. It looks like an eight lying on its side.

This is a loop the loop.

This move is called a complete roll.

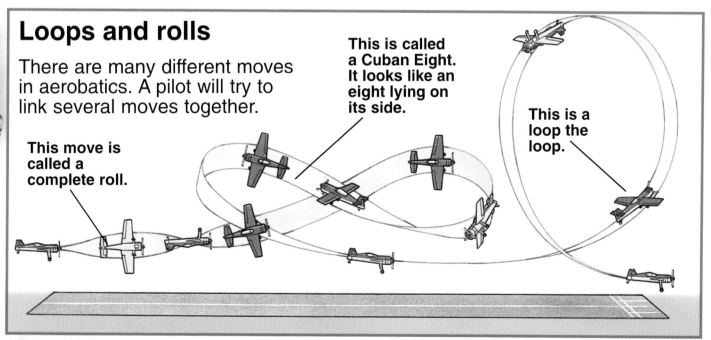

Formation teams

Flying close together in groups is called formation flying. Military planes often fly in groups for protection. Many air forces have special formation teams. These perform exciting displays at airshows.

The Blue Angels

The Blue Angels is a very famous formation team. It is made up of pilots and planes from the United States Navy. They first flew in 1946 in planes with propellers. They now use fast jets called FA-18 Hornets.

This plane is leading the others. They are all flying straight up in formation.

The pilot inside this plane is called the Flight Leader.

The cockpit has room for just one pilot.

There is often no more than one metre (3ft) between the planes.

The bright yellow and blue markings make the planes stand out in the sky.

Famous formations

Many formations have been given names. Here are three formations used by the British Red Arrows team. This team flies with nine planes.

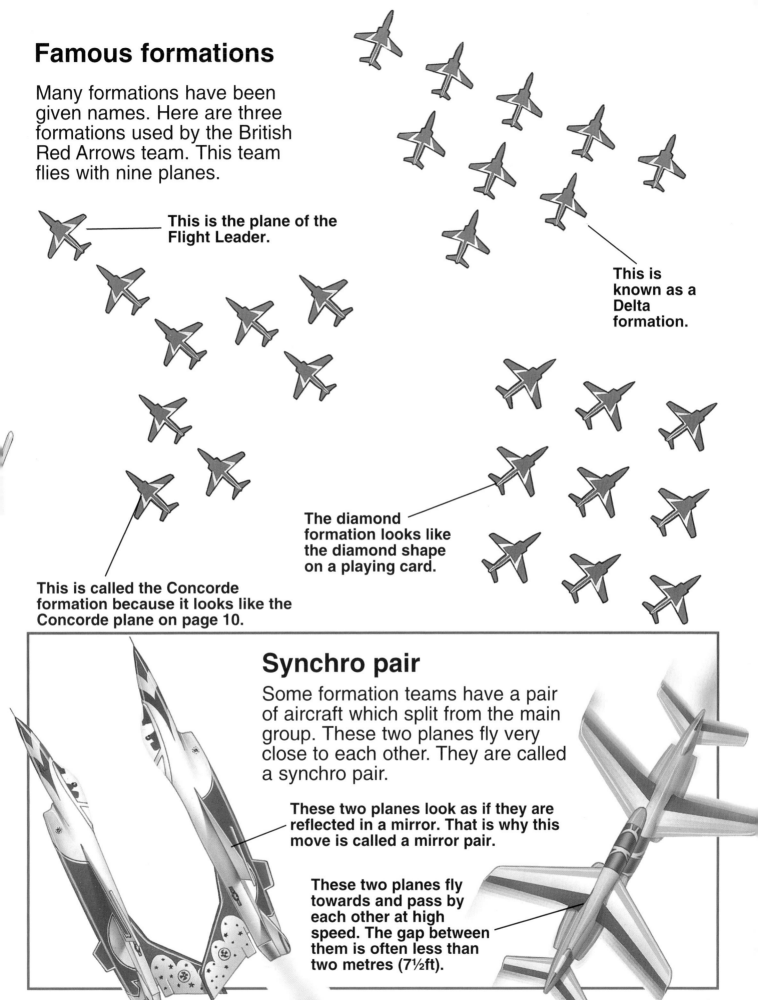

This is the plane of the **Flight Leader.**

This is known as a **Delta formation.**

The **diamond formation** looks like the diamond shape on a playing card.

This is called the **Concorde formation** because it looks like the Concorde plane on page 10.

Synchro pair

Some formation teams have a pair of aircraft which split from the main group. These two planes fly very close to each other. They are called a synchro pair.

These two planes look as if they are reflected in a mirror. That is why this move is called a **mirror pair.**

These two planes fly towards and pass by each other at high speed. The gap between them is often less than two metres (7½ft).

Giant helicopters

Helicopters come in many sizes. The smallest hold just a pilot and nothing else. The largest can carry many people or big machines.

This helicopter doesn't have a tail rotor to help it turn (see page 5). Instead, the pilot changes the speed of the two main rotors to move left or right.

The cockpit holds a crew of three.

This helicopter can hold 44 passengers.

Here is one of this helicopter's two engines.

The three crane hooks are for lifting heavy things.

This helicopter is 30m (100ft) long.

This searchlight can be used to look for things on the ground at night.

Boeing Chinook

This helicopter is used by armies to transport soldiers and vehicles. Some airlines also use Chinooks to carry passengers to places that are hard to reach, such as oil rigs.

This bulldozer is being flown to a rescue area. It can quickly clear away mud and stones.

24

Refuelling

Helicopter

Tanker

OH 2301

301

This basket helps guide the pipes together.

Fuel flows through these pipes.

Helicopter's refuelling probe

Tanker hose

When refuelling stops, the pipes come apart.

Filling up the fuel tank while flying is called in-flight refuelling. A tanker plane and helicopter join fuel pipes. Then the tanker pumps fuel out.

Sikorsky Skycrane

This is an unusual giant helicopter. It doesn't carry heavy loads inside its body. Instead it flies along with a large container underneath.

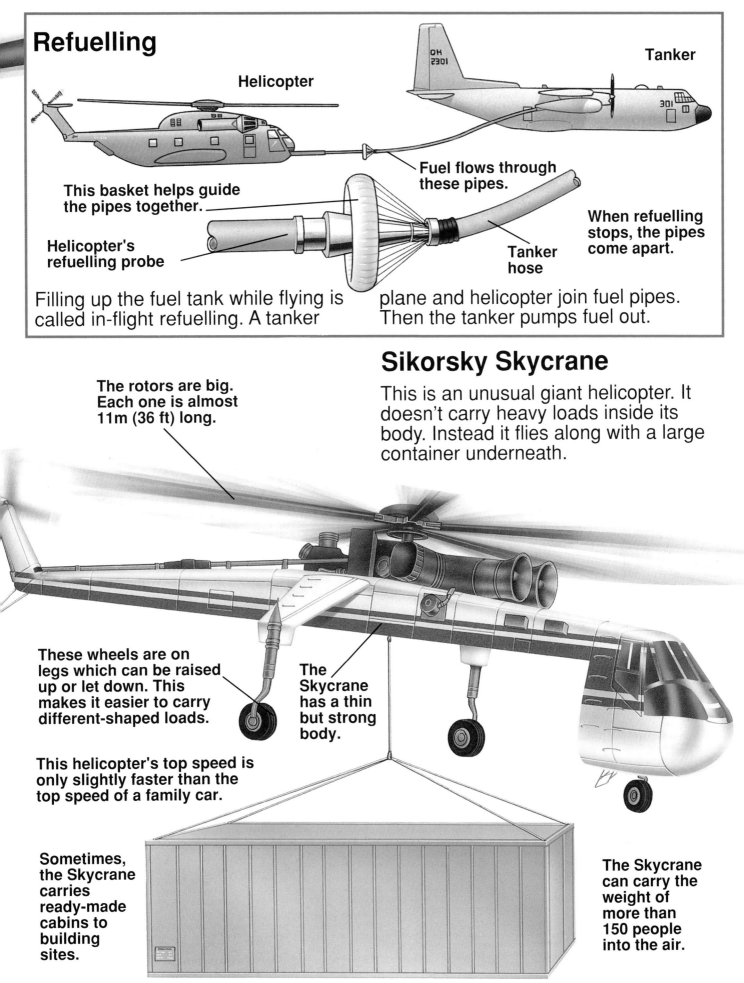

The rotors are big. Each one is almost 11m (36 ft) long.

These wheels are on legs which can be raised up or let down. This makes it easier to carry different-shaped loads.

The Skycrane has a thin but strong body.

This helicopter's top speed is only slightly faster than the top speed of a family car.

Sometimes, the Skycrane carries ready-made cabins to building sites.

The Skycrane can carry the weight of more than 150 people into the air.

25

Swing-wing planes

Some planes have wings that move. They are called swing-wings. The wings stick out for take off and landing. This makes the plane easier for the pilot to control. When the wings swing back, the plane can go faster.

There is a crew of two, a pilot and a weapons operator.

The crew members sit on special ejection seats (see right).

F-14 Tomcat

The F-14 Tomcat is used mainly by the United States Navy. Its swing-wings help it fly very fast. It has a top speed of over 2,400km/h (1,500mph).

Here you can see inside the cockpit.

Panavia Tornado

This military plane is built by companies from Germany, Italy and Britain. It can be used to drop bombs or to fight other planes in the air.

This circular joint is called the pivot bearing. The wings can swing around it.

The pilot sits in the front of the cockpit.

The navigator sits behind the pilot. The navigator is the person who works out where to fly.

With its fuel tanks full, the Tornado can fly up to 3,600km (2,200 miles) in one trip.

These wings have moved forward to slow the plane down for take off or landing.

With its wings back, this plane's top speed is over 2,300km/h (1,425mph).

These wings are swept back for speed.

NE

This part helps increase the engine's power. It is called an afterburner because it burns some of the waste gases after they have left the engine.

The Tomcat weighs more than three Harrier planes (see pages 12 and 13).

The Tomcat's tailplanes tilt up and down. They act like big elevators (see page 2).

Ejection seat

Ejection seats throw pilots clear of planes that are about to crash.

Ejection seats work in three stages. First, strong explosives blow the cockpit canopy off.

Then, more explosives fire the seat into the air. This throws a pilot safely away from the plane.

Once clear of the plane, the seat falls away and a parachute carries the pilot safely to the ground.

Crazy planes

Planes come in all shapes and sizes. Many planes look similar and do similar jobs. But there are a few strange planes that are quite different. Here are four crazy planes.

Gee Bee racer

This plane was built for racing. It has a massive engine squeezed into a tiny body. The plane won many races in the 1930s.

The engine in the Gee Bee racer is large and very powerful.

It has a top speed of 497 km/h (308 mph).

The plane is just over 5m (17ft) long. That's only a little bit longer than an ordinary family car.

This side panel is a door. It is where the pilot gets in.

These metal wires help to support the wing. They are called bracing wires.

Covers over the wheels help the air flow smoothly past. This makes the plane go faster.

This tiny wheel at the back of the plane is called the tail wheel.

NR2100

Gee Bee

Rotabuggy

This is a 1940s jeep with some helicopter parts added. It was meant to be towed behind a big plane.

The rotors keep the rotabuggy up in the air.

Inflatoplane

This amazing plane first flew in 1953. It came as a kit in a 2m (6½ft) long box. It was made to be dropped from planes to soldiers on the ground. They could then put the parts together and fly it.

The cockpit held two people.

The wings were made of rubber and were pumped up with a footpump.

Optica

This modern plane has a cockpit you can see out of in all directions. The plane is used for taking photographs in the air and for watching traffic on the road.

These join the tail to the wing. They are called booms.

The engine drives a large fan around in here. This pushes the plane forward.

The cockpit is made of a see-through plastic.

Stealth planes

Some of the latest warplanes use special shapes and paints to make them difficult to see. These are called stealth planes. This stealth plane is the Lockheed F117A.

This plane has a number of nicknames. These are Black Jet, Nighthawk, Frisbee and Wobbly Goblin.

This plane has just landed. The small parachute helps pull the main parachute out of the plane.

The body and wings of the plane are mainly made of strong but light metals.

The large main parachute helps the plane slow down when it lands.

This plane has a wingspan of just under 14m (45ft).

How does radar see planes?

This is a radar dish. It sends and receives radar signals.

Signals bounce off plane.

The dish collects the signals as they bounce back.

Radar equipment, joined to a big radar dish, sends special radio signals through the air. These bounce back if they hit anything solid.

The radar dish then collects the signals that bounce back. People who work the radar can tell if the signals have bounced off a plane.

Stealth and the F117A

All of the F117A's stealth features help confuse enemies' radar systems. They make the radar think that the plane is not a plane but something else, like a flock of birds.

The plane is covered in a special substance called R.A.M. This stands for Radar Absorbent Material. R.A.M. soaks up the radar signals so they do not bounce back.

The cockpit seats one person only.

Stealth planes are usually painted black. This makes the planes harder to see at night.

These flat surfaces, all poking out at different angles are called facets. They help to scatter the radar beams.

The front nosewheel goes up into the plane here.

This fighter plane first flew in 1981 but was kept secret until 1988.

Stealth bomber

This is the Northrop B2 bomber. It is made in the United States and first flew in 1989.

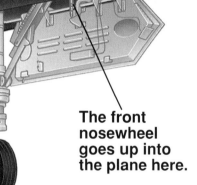

Because of its shape, it is known as a flying wing.

It has a very big wingspan of over 52m (170ft).

The B2 has four engines, two on either side of the cockpit.

It can fly 8,000km (5,000 miles) in one trip. That's almost as far as from London to Los Angeles.

Index